IMAGES
of America

ROCKLIN

IMAGES
of America

ROCKLIN

Carmel Barry-Schweyer
and Alycia S. Alvarez

ARCADIA
PUBLISHING

Published by Arcadia Publishing
Charleston, South Carolina

Library of Congress Catalog Card Number: 2005922451

For all general information contact Arcadia Publishing at:
Telephone 843-853-2070
Fax 843-853-0044
E-mail sales@arcadiapublishing.com
For customer service and orders:
Toll-Free 1-888-313-2665

Visit us on the Internet at www.arcadiapublishing.com

CONTENTS

ACKNOWLEDGMENTS

The authors would like to thank Ron Petersen, Roy Ruhkala, Jean Day, and Bob and Sharon Balmain for their assistance. The photographs in this book are courtesy of the Rocklin Historical Society and Placer County Department of Museums.

This book is dedicated to my mother, Maxine Lucia Ammon Barry (1920–2005).
Her strength, love, and encouragement has guided me through my life.
I miss her deeply; she was the wind beneath my wings.

—Carmel Barry-Schweyer

INTRODUCTION

The Nisenan group of Maidu Indians occupied what is now called Placer County, west of the crest of the Sierra Nevada Mountains to the Sacramento River. The rolling oak woodland in the vicinity of Rocklin, with the creek running through Secret Ravine, was an ideal location for a village. Depressions worn in granite outcroppings are still visible where Native American women spent many afternoons grinding acorns into meal. The Nisenan way of life would change forever in 1849.

The 1848 discovery of gold in California by James Marshall caused the largest voluntary migration in the history of the world. Fortune seekers by the thousands came to the foothills of the Sierra Nevada Mountains. They worked the rivers and streams from their headwaters in the mountains to the Sacramento Valley. Miners worked along Secret Ravine in what is now Placer County, from the present day communities of Newcastle to Roseville.

In 1852, James Bolton, a miner and native of Ireland, acquired 160 acres of land which including what would become the town site of Rocklin. The Central Pacific Railroad cut though his land and reached the town site in 1864. The first load of freight hauled on the new railroad was 30 tons of granite from Rocklin quarries in March 1864. Bolton laid out the town site in 1866, and Rocklin grew due to the railroad and the cluster of quarries surrounding the area.

By 1865, approximately seven families lived in the Rocklin area. The Dixon family, Dr. Page, James Bolton, the Van Trees, Mr. Frame, John Glindcamp, John Conner, and the workers at the Brigham and Hawes Quarry were early settlers. Daniel and Rebecca Van Trees operated a boardinghouse. Bishop and Hawes established the Purdy House for their quarry workers and Frame owned a small general store.

Rocklin saw an influx of Irish immigrants who worked for the railroad and the quarries by the 1870s. In the 1880s, immigrants from Finland settled in the area, and one Finn, John Mantyla, is credited with drawing them to Rocklin. He arrived in the 1870s and wrote letters home encouraging family and friends to come to this wonderful part of California. By 1890, the Finns made up a majority of the population.

In 1867, the town of Rocklin began to take shape. George W. Dunster opened a general merchandise store. Joseph West Bleden and Christopher Dalton each opened saloons. Daniel Van Trees died that year and his widow, Rebecca, sold the boardinghouse on the corner of Front and E Streets to A.A. Alexander of Folsom. By May of 1867, the Auburn newspaper *Stars and Stripes* reported that "some 40 or 50 buildings were estimated to have been built or in the process of being built." By this time, the railroad roundhouse had been completed and track laid.

The granite industry was blossoming by the late 1860s, and by the 1890s more than 22 quarries were operating in the Rocklin vicinity. Granite quarries and the railroad became the main employers in the predominantly male town. Thousands of tons of granite from Rocklin quarries were shipped as far away as Pearl Harbor, Washington, D.C., Fresno, San Francisco, Washington, Nevada, and San Jose. Granite was used for ornate carved pediments and pillars on buildings, curbing for city streets, riprap for docks and breakwaters, and blocks to build bridges and buildings.

Rocklin had numerous saloons, boardinghouses, barber shops, and bathhouses by the 1870s. In the following decade, Rocklin had two hotels and a boardinghouse, nine saloons, and five stores. That era also saw completion of the Masonic Hall, which served as the home for the Brotherhood of Locomotive Firemen, the International Order of Odd Fellows Lodge, and the Legion of Honor. There were three churches and a school, and a library association formed.

In addition to saloons and fraternal organizations, Rocklin residents had a variety of other options for filling leisure time. The pond at Hathaway's Quarry filled with swimmers in the hot summer months. Workman's Grove was a popular spot for picnics and dances, and young and old also danced until the small hours at Grants Hall and Exchange Hall. A brass band organized to entertain at such gatherings. The racetrack, which featured both horse and dog racing, was a popular place to spend the afternoon.

The early 1890s were scarred by a series of fires and a Pullman strike that crippled the railroad and shut down the quarries for a time. Yet the citizens of Rocklin seemed undaunted by the tragedies. They rebuilt larger and more substantial buildings and the quarries rebounded. After the turn to the century, the stone Barudoni Building and the Fireman's Hall on Front Street and Finn Hall on present-day Rocklin Road (originally Granite Street) were constructed.

Rocklin bustled with 300 railroad employees. And almost half of them worked in the railroad roundhouse servicing approximately 1,200 locomotives each month. However, the Southern Pacific Railroad dealt a crushing blow to Rocklin when it announced that the roundhouse would be moved to Roseville by 1908. The roundhouse turntable was removed in 1910 and the building itself torn down. At that point many houses and businesses moved along with their residents and proprietors from Rocklin to Roseville. It was estimated that 100 buildings would eventually relocate to Roseville, and by 1909 over 40 residences had already been moved with seven more buildings lost to a fire in that year.

In the first decade of the 20th century, Rocklin lost almost half of its population, bringing it to 1,026 by 1910. As if that weren't enough, yet another huge fire in 1914 destroyed everything between Barudoni's and Trott's Hotel on Front Street. The following year, a strike shut down most quarries from June to January.

In the 1920s, Rocklin's California Granite Company found itself occupied with supplying building material for the Bank of Italy in San Francisco. The Ruhkala brothers bought California Granite in 1935 and renamed it the Union Granite Company. Another large quarry, the Delano, was sold to the city to use as a dump.

Little physical evidence is left today of Rocklin's vigorous granite industry. The once prominent railroad roundhouse is but a pile of rubble with trees and weeds covering its remains. The Union Granite Company's derricks are visible as one drives along Pacific Avenue or Rocklin Road. They stand like sentinels of the past, waiting for recognition of their importance in the making of Rocklin. A new way of life has adapted to the relics of the old. Subdivisions now nestle around old quarry holes as new immigrants to Rocklin use them as backdrops or ponds for their residential landscape.

One

RAILROAD

This group posed in front of Central Pacific Locomotive No. 1535 around 1900. Pictured, from left to right, are Jim Kelly, Jimmie Jordan, Ed Jordan, Jim Lee, Ben Collins, Will Landis, ? La Shill, Jim Hurley, Charles Hindrich, and Ralph Smith. Ed Jordan went on to become a foreman for the Pacific Fruit Express at Roseville.

Jakii Sanduuto was said to have run Southern Pacific Locomotive No. 1002, used for switching at the busy Rocklin Roundhouse. Central Pacific Railroad came to Rocklin in 1864, and the roundhouse was eventually built in 1866.

In this photo, Engine No. 75 makes its way up Cape Horn in 1875. Trains traveling from Sacramento up to the summit at Truckee would begin pulling about 35 cars. At Rocklin, the number of cars dwindled down to 18, and, in Colfax, more cars were removed. Often, two engines were needed to power up the steep incline.

Charles Trott became an engineer for the Central Pacific Railroad in 1873. His old engine, C.P. No. 46, is pictured here *c.* 1890. Charles's father, Sam, owned Trott's Hotel in Rocklin. Sam was also a railroad man at one time, and his hotel was popular with railroad workers.

Early residents of Rocklin stand in front of locomotive No. 374. Pictured, from left to right, are (front row) unidentified, Don Grant, Dave Pease, Mr. Tilbert, Mrs. Tilbert, Edith Hathaway Mast, and Mrs. Tom Nofend with son; (back row) unidentified, unidentified, and Mrs. Tom Nofend's other son.

Two of the men in this picture are identified as Henry Curran and L.B. Ketcham. All four men are standing on a caboose identified as Southern Pacific No. 65. In 1891, the Rocklin depot burned down. John Sweeney was the depot agent and, in fact, built the depot and leased it to the railroad company.

In this c. 1890 photo, a tender for the Central Pacific Locomotive No. 177 is filled to the brim with cords of wood. Wood-burning locomotives could use up to 16 cords of wood to get over the summit. The railroad and mining industries were responsible for stripping bare many of the landscapes across Placer County.

12

A group of young boys and railroad workers stand in front of the Rocklin station around 1891. The Rocklin station sign directs people to trains bound in the direction of San Francisco and Ogden, Utah. The Central Pacific Railroad reached Ogden in March of 1869.

The Colfax–Sacramento Local heads east through Rocklin around 1912. Joe Hackett, in the horse and buggy, was the postmaster for Rocklin. In the background, on the right, is Burchard Hotel and Porter's Saloon. In 1914, a fire destroyed these buildings.

This c. 1900 photo shows No. 1986, which was operated and maintained by engineer Christian Rasmussen from 1893 until 1901. Rasmussen lived in Rocklin on the corner of Emery and Second Streets. Local newspapers reported that Rocklin's neighborhoods had an issue with hobos brought in by the train traffic. There was also a report in 1904 that a young lady who was visiting Rocklin was walking along the railroad tracks when a brakeman threatened to "cut her in two." She ran for her life.

Although the date of this picture is debatable—1868 or 1885—it does inarguably picture a 10-wheeler on a 55-foot turntable at the Rocklin Roundhouse. The roundhouse, like Rocklin, fell victim to many fires. In 1869, the woodshed caught fire, and in 1873 the roundhouse caught fire and destroyed 10 locomotives with their tenders. The 10 locomotives and tenders were worth about $30,000.

Piled in the foreground is fuel for the wood-burning locomotives. This picture, taken around 1875, captures the arduous work that woodcutters performed to help keep the trains running. In 1869, the woodsheds that could store up to 25,000 cords of wood caught fire. Much of the wood was burned, and a fire train from Sacramento had to put out the fire.

The Rocklin Roundhouse had approximately 25 stalls for storage of large, wood-burning locomotives. A locomotive tender, or firebox, contained the wood needed to travel up to the summit. A cord of wood is a pile of 2 feet logs, 4 feet wide, 4 feet high, and 128 feet long.

One of the last locomotives at the Rocklin Roundhouse sits on the turntable. This picture reveals a group of men standing in front of No. 2679 around 1908. In 1905, Rocklin citizens were excited to learn that Central Pacific Railroad had plans to build a new roundhouse. However their excitement was extinguished when Roseville was named as the new site.

Funeral Notice

〜•〜

DIED--At Rocklin, April 18, 1908,

The Rocklin Round House

A Native of California.
Aged 42 Years.

〜•〜

. . . FUNERAL . . .

Funeral services will be held at Porter's Hall,

Saturday Evening, April 18, 1908, at 8. P. M.

PALLBEARERS—J. Curran, J. B. Garity, J. Collins, Ed Folger.

HONORARY PALLBEARERS—L. W. McCarl, J. E. Arnel, A. Burke, T. Ronan.

〜•〜

Friends and acquaintances are respectfully invited to attend the funeral, where refreshments will be served.

Drays and Wheelbarrows will be ordered at 12 o'clock, Midnight.

〜•〜

Interment--Roseville.

N. B. The Machinists will not be responsible for the Boilermakers' actions.

The people of Rocklin, upset by the loss of their beloved roundhouse, held a funeral for their departed friend. It was sad news, indeed. Hundreds of people moved from Rocklin to Roseville, some taking their homes with them. But by 1910, with the help of the growing quarry industry, Rocklin recovered from the loss of the roundhouse.

Two

QUARRIES AND
QUARRYMEN

On May 20, 1919, Southern Pacific switch engine No. 1152 fell into the quarry when the ground beneath the tracks along the edge of the quarry gave way due to the weight of the engine. Visible in the background is the shed of the Pacific Granite Company, also known as Copp's Quarry.

Another view of the Southern Pacific switch engine shows that it stopped about two feet from the 40-foot deep water hole. The water had to pumped out of the hole and the engine taken apart to haul it out of the quarry pit. Apparently the engineer was not hurt in this accident, as the newspaper article did not mention any injuries.

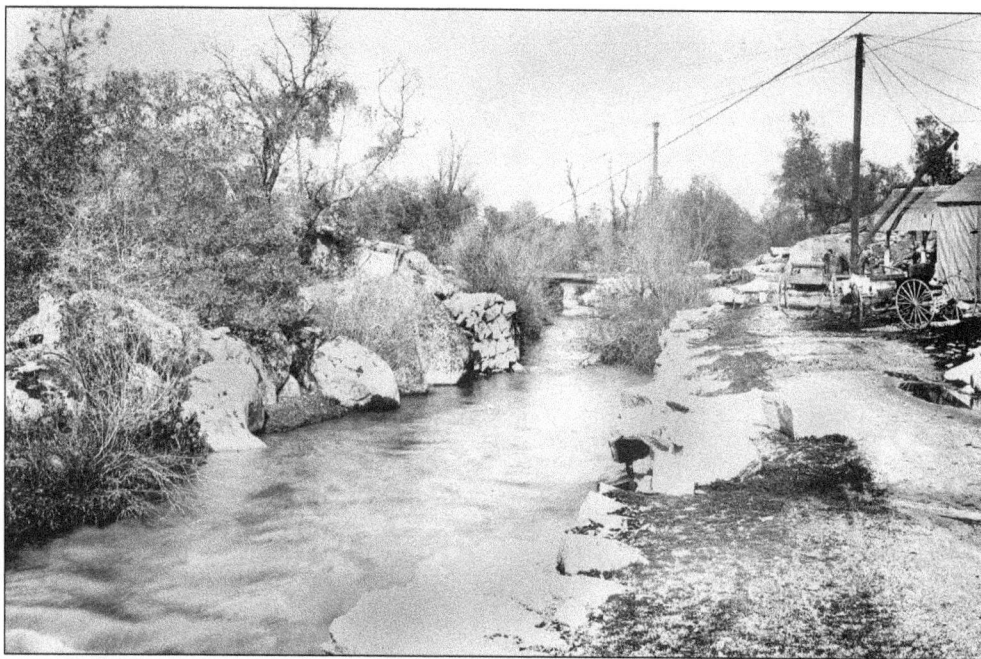

Copp's Quarry derrick, on the right in this photo, borders Secret Ravine. In the distance is the railroad bridge used to cross the ravine. The area was known as Saintula's swimming hole and picnic ground. In 1900, there was a swinging bridge on cables for the wagons to cross the creek. Notice the buggies on the right.

Small quarry operations that did not have steam engines to hoist the granite out of the pit used a windlass, or whim, powered by a horse, such as this one at Copp's Quarry. The horse is attached to a horizontal wooden boom that turns the vertical timber as the horse walks around in a circle. As it turns, the timber winds a cable on the spool attached at its bottom. The cable is visible at the bottom of the spool. As the cable winds around the spool it hoists the stones out of the quarry.

Don Grant is standing on the wagon in A.D. Hathaway's quarry in the 1880s. Also identified in this picture are Mr. Hathaway and John Lonergan Sr., who are loading granite onto the wagon. Hathaway leased the quarry, including 40 acres from the Pacific Granite Company, for $1 plus $2 for rough stone and $7.50 for dimension stone per carload. This was originally the Brigham and Hawes Quarry, begun in 1864 and located on the west side of Pacific Avenue.

Griffith Griffith, pioneer quarryman of Placer County, opened this quarry in Rocklin in 1878. First known as Granite Stone Quarry, it was eventually purchased by Ira Lemuel Delano and became known as Delano Quarry. But its official name was the Rocklin Granite Company. Quarry sheds are in the center, with two derricks at either side.

The Southern Pacific Railroad spur can be seen cutting through the quarry yard. Spur tracks ran along both sides of the quarry. In the right center of the picture, two men are guiding a rough-cut stone hanging from the boom at Delano Quarry.

This view of Delano Quarry shows a rough-cut stone being hoisted out of the quarry under two booms at center right. At far right center, a railroad flat car is waiting for a load. In 1891, the quarry was 150 feet by 250 feet and 100 feet deep. Five steam derricks, each with a capability of hoisting 25 tons, were in operation.

The size and depth of Delano Quarry is demonstrated in this picture. Three men work in the bottom of the 100-foot pit. One in the bottom center stands on a boulder and two are working on a boulder at the right center. Early operations that Delano Quarry would eventually surpass in productivity included: A.D. Hathaway (30 men), Brigham and Hawes, (30 to 40 men), Quinn Quarry, (25 men), and State Capitol Quarry, (28 men).

These men are working in the cutting shed at Delano Quarry c. 1895. The crane running on a track on the horizontal timbers in the back of the shed is for lifting and moving large stones. Two pulleys can be seen hanging down from the track.

Three men stop working in the blacksmith shop to pose for a picture at Delano Quarry, located north of Interstate 80 and west of Rocklin Road. It was used as the city dump for many years. Today, a hotel occupies the site.

Men working the overhead crane in the cutting shed of Delano Quarry pose for a picture c. 1900. Ira Delano came from Maine to California in the late 1860s, and mined for gold in the Auburn and Colfax areas before coming to Rocklin. He bought the quarry from the heirs of Griffith Griffith for $13,000.

In the 1890s, George Willard, the oxen driver, is pictured hauling granite from Delano Quarry. Michael Kelley of Rattlesnake Bar hauled granite blocks from the Rocklin quarry for the railroad from 1864 until 1867. He was said to have eight yoke of the "largest oxen in this part of California."

The Delano Quarry crew assembles in front of the shed to pose for a picture. In 1891, Ira Delano filed articles of incorporation for the Rocklin Granite Company. The board of directors held 500 shares of stock with a value of $100 per share. Delano held 250 shares, Hiram Tubbs 120 shares, George S. Lackie and F.W. Henshaw 5 shares each, and D. Edward Collins 120 shares.

Stonecutters gather in the shed for a picture at Delano Quarry, c. 1890. The granite boom of the 1870s—caused by the need for granite curbing in urban areas—had declined by the 1880s. By April of 1880, Taylor Quarry was the only quarry operating until the following October, when Hathaway's Quarry reopened. At the end of the decade, Griffith Quarry (later Delano), John Taylor Quarry, Russian Quarry, and John Grant Quarry reopened.

The crew gathers in the shed of Delano Quarry for a picture. The only men identified in this picture are Colin Hislop (front row, seated second from left), Raphel Ponce (fifth from left), and Jim Fisher (to his right holding the square).

Quarrymen pose for a group picture in the shed at Delano Quarry. In the 1890s, four trains transported granite from Rocklin daily to construct the Crocker Bank vault in Sacramento, the Hibernia Bank and Flood vault in San Francisco, until they were completed.

A group of stonecutters gather in the cutting shed for a picture. Only two are identified, Alfred Nassi (on the far left) and Gabriel Alexson (on the back left with the sun partially on his face). Gabriel Alexson came to Rocklin from Finland and was naturalized in 1894.

Wickman-Alexson Quarry was located on Winding Lane at Lost Avenue. This 1910 view shows the huge size of the derrick and boom on the right. The spur track for transporting stone can be seen in the center, curving to the left.

The crew of Wickman-Alexson Quarry poses in the cutting shed for a picture. The stone cutting saw can be seen in the right center of the picture. The picture is taken looking south, and the Rocklin cemetery is in the background on the right.

A Placer Granite Company crew, numbering more than 40, stands in front of the cutting shed c. 1912. The back of this photo is labeled, "Vic Wickman Quarry looking northwest." Victor Wickman came to Rocklin from Finland in 1902 and became naturalized in 1911.

This view shows Wickman-Alexson Quarry as it looked in the 1920s. The cutting shed is visible to the left of the derricks. Note the ladders in the pit on the right side of the picture. Nikolas Alexson first started in the quarry business with his father, Gabriel, Nico Palo, and Sanfred Wallen. He later formed a partnership with Victor Wickman.

The Pernu Quarry, officially known as the Capitol Granite Company, was originally owned by S.D. Smith and later by John Nay Taylor. Smith supplied granite from this quarry for the California state capitol building from March 1865 until 1870, when the decision was made to continue the building with less expensive brick construction. The name of the company was changed to the California Granite Company when Adolph Pernu purchased it.

Three men stand below the boom in the center of this picture. The Methodist church is visible near the edge of the California Granite Company quarry in the right center. The church was located on Rocklin Road.

Rocklin stonecutters work on a stone at Front Quarry, also known as the California Granite Company quarry. In 1907, Pernu filed articles of incorporation with 50,000 shares of stock. Pernu held 25,010 shares; Hector N. Bernieri and Duilio Tosi held 12,490 shares each; and Hilma Pernu and Isidor Levison each held 5 shares. By 1915, Pernu held 49,990 shares. H. Pernu held one share, and A.W. Grindell held two shares.

This north-looking view of Front Quarry shows two quarrymen in the lower right cutting and securing cables around a giant stone. The pulley for the hoist can be seen in the upper left, to the left of the ladder.

Front Quarry is pictured here in about 1900 with three quarrymen. Two quarrymen in the center watch a stone as it is hoisted out of the hole in the left center. The ladders on the far upper right of the picture show how the quarrymen had to get into and out of the quarry pits.

Pictured c. 1908 is Front Quarry, looking south from San Francisco Street. Work in the quarries was dangerous. In February 1912, Nick Maki was killed after losing his balance stepping across a cut while carrying a heavy pipe. He fell 30 feet to the bottom of the pit.

Workers pose for a picture at Front Quarry c. 1905. By 1904, more than 500 men—a majority of them Finnish—were employed in 22 Rocklin quarries. They were paid comparatively high wages, and the Stonecutter's Union was very strong. Stonecutters earned $4 for a 9-hour day, while quarrymen were paid $2.15 a day.

This 1908 view of the California Granite Company quarry, taken from Rocklin Road looking southwest, shows the sheds and a portion of the pit. The picture was taken from Rocklin Road near the Labor Temple or old Methodist Church.

Emma Abner (about six years old), and Matt Ruhkala are pictured in 1912 at Ruhkala's Quarry, now under Interstate 80. Matt Ruhkala, born in Finland, arrived in Rocklin in 1889. He married Eva Ericsen and had 11 children. In 1904, he started the Union Granite Company.

Pictured here c. 1915 is Front Quarry looking north, with the church in the right top of the photo. The church, located on Rocklin Road, was torn down in the 1920s to make way for a new church.

A.M. Grindell looks at plans in the California Granite Company office in 1912. Statuary photographs hang on the wall over the desk, and just to the left of the desk on the wall is a "first aid cabinet."

Anita Grindell and Helmi Pernu posed for this picture in the California Granite Company office in April 1912. An electric light bulb hangs over the typewriter, and an old Burroughs adding machine sits on a desk in the right center.

Two men in the center foreground are walking from the cutting shed into the quarry of the California Granite Company in Rocklin. The white building in the right center of the picture is a steam bath, and to the left is the Kesti house.

Abner, Gideon, Benjamin, and Rueben Ruhkala purchased the Union Granite Company quarry, previously the California Granite Company quarry, in 1935. This quarry was one of the largest producers in Rocklin.

Henry Stone and Alfred Huhtala stand by the gang saw in this c. 1920 picture. Henry worked as a polisher. The California Granite Company won the contract for supplying granite to the new Bank of Italy building in San Francisco. This job provided work for 85 men for one year.

Matt Ruhkala Quarry on Ruhkala Road is featured in this 1930 photo looking southwest. Ruhkala purchased the A.O. Wickman quarry in 1919. Granite from Rocklin quarries was used for construction of Ft. Lewis, Washington, and for the naval station at Pearl Harbor.

Matt Ruhkala is loading the truck with cut stone in 1928. By 1920, the population of Rocklin was 643, and the majority were Finnish. Only seven quarries were in business by 1928. In 1977, crushed quartz from Rocklin was used for the Transamerica Pyramid in San Francisco.

A stone is being loaded onto a Wells Transportation, Inc. truck from Reno, Nevada. The stone is to be used for a drilling contest in Wells, Nevada, in 1934. Roy Ruhkala is in the truck wearing a white hat, and Ben Ruhkala is on the ground. The sign on the stone reads, "Union Granite Co. Ruhkala Bros. Rocklin, Calif."

Shown here in 1936 is the Front Quarry looking west in the shed. Pictured, from left to right, are John Walgren (standing at the side of the shed), Ben Ruhkala (working on stone), Roy and Abner Ruhkala (at the end of the granite slab), and Jerry Wuottiat (to the far right of the shed).

Seen here is Alex Water's quarry that later became Pernu's Back Quarry. The Sierra Lakes Mobile Home Park clubhouse is now located where the man in the picture is standing. A portion of the old quarry is now a lake behind the clubhouse.

The Hebuck Quarry was located on South Grove Street. This picture was taken looking east toward South Grove Street. Approximately 30 quarries were operating in the 1890s in the Rocklin area. More than 60 quarry operations have been worked in Rocklin.

Posing here at the Kesti Quarry *c.* 1900 are, from left to right, Otto Kesti, Eli Aho, Charles Hendrickson, ? Sokra, unidentified, E. Marttila, and unidentified. Bachelor quarrymen who lived in company houses worked full time, while married men, or men who boarded elsewhere, did not get full time work. This situation caused a weeklong strike in 1904, and the Stonecutters Union voted to impose a $5 fine on every member who boarded in his employers boardinghouse.

Peter Johnson, Matt Oja, Michael Johnson, Albert Johnson, Oscar Elliason, and Sasti Moinen pause from their work to have a picture taken. They are each holding tools including sledgehammers, drill bits, a square, and a chisel.

A quarryman perches on an overhead crane ready to lift a slab of granite, while three others look on. Granite shipped from Rocklin to Sequoia National Park was used to construct stone bridges in 1931. In the late 1930s, contractors used granite from Rocklin for many summer homes and hotels in the Lake Tahoe area.

This c. 1905 photo shows a belt-drive polishing machine and bed inside the cutting shed. Many of the small quarries provided granite curbing for cities like Sacramento, Stockton, and San Francisco. Rocklin quarries also provided granite paving blocks for city streets.

Ivar, Richard, and Oscar Kesti are shown here in the shed at their quarry c. 1910, when Rocklin could boast 22 operating quarries. During the following decade, granite was shipped for the courthouse in Reno, Nevada, the bell tower at the University of California, Berkeley, the Sacramento County Jail, and the tunnel under the railroad tracks in Newcastle.

In this c. 1898 photo looking southwest, three of the derricks of Wickman-Alexson Quarry are visible. Also pictured are the cutting shed, stone shed, air compressor, shed, and office. The Ruhkala home is in the center background.

Here, stonecutters are at work in the shed. In 1915, granite workers had a strike for higher wages. They wanted $5.60 for stonecutters and $3.75 for quarrymen for an eight-hour day. Quarries were shut down for over six months before the strike was finally settled in January 1916. By the time the strike was over, most workers had left town, which resulted in many quarries going out of business.

Listed on the back of this September 1911 picture are William Nicoli, Albert Hollonen, John Beasmore, Tom Owens, Maurice Grindell, George Willard, ? Owens, Ira Allen, Jim Fisher, Eric Lilhtola, Tom Sheehan, Colin Hislop, Jim Ryan, Ira Wilson, Leonard Newkirk, Alice Newkirk, and Sam Rinaldi.

42

Finnish quarrymen stop work to have their picture taken c. 1915. The man at the top is identified as Mr. Niskala. Granite from Rocklin quarries was used for building the docks at Fort Mason, San Francisco, Mare Island, Hawaii, and the Philippines.

Pictured here are a quarry hole and engine house. Tons of Rocklin granite was shipped to San Jose, Fresno, Monterey, Oakland, Reno, and Tonopah, Nevada, as well as Sacramento and San Francisco. Many public buildings and churches throughout the West were built of Rocklin granite.

Hugh slabs of granite are being loaded onto a Southern Pacific railroad car on one of the spur tracks. Thirty tons of granite made up the first freight hauled by the Central Pacific Railroad (later the Southern Pacific Railroad, and now Union Pacific Railroad) when the tracks were completed from Sacramento to Rocklin.

In this 1906 photo, a train hauls granite from San Francisco to Colma. The brakeman in the right rear of the wagon is Charlie Tronoff. After the 1906 earthquake, most of the cemeteries in San Francisco were moved to Colma because the board of supervisors outlawed all new burials in the city or county of San Francisco. Rocklin granite was used both in reconstruction of buildings and streets and also for monuments in the cemeteries in Colma.

Granite from Rocklin's California Granite Company was used to construct the Matson Mausoleum in a cemetery in Colma, south of San Francisco.

California Granite Company created this design for the Bank of Italy, later Bank of America, in San Francisco at Powell and Market Street in 1920.

Howard Scribner (inside the truck) and Charles J. Tronoff (standing by the rear wheel) pose for a picture with a finished granite carving at the California Granite Company shop at Eighth and Bryant Streets in San Francisco. The granite on the truck is the piece for the Bank of Italy.

A crane hoists the granite work done by Mr. Laasko, a stonecutter who worked for the California Granite Company of Rocklin.

John Tuta stands next to a piece of ornate stonework ready to be displayed at the Panama Pacific International Exposition in San Francisco in 1915. The stone piece is a capital for one of the many ornate buildings that were constructed for the exposition.
Only a portion of the Palace of Fine Arts remains.

Pictured here is a beautiful example of the exquisite work done by the Rocklin quarries. Monuments and funerary statues were a mainstay for some quarries.

The Campanile at the University of California, Berkeley, was made from Rocklin granite and completed in 1914. The structure still stands as the focal point for the campus. Emile Benard, with John Galen Howard as supervising architect, designed the plan for the campus.

Quarrymen gather for a picture at the McGilvrey-Raymond Granite Company shed in eastern Madera County, where many Rocklin quarrymen worked when activity at Rocklin quarries slowed. The men are standing and kneeling on a piece of granite that is 32 feet long by 3.5 feet wide and 1 foot thick.

Three

COMMERCE

This photo shows Front Street from the corner of Granite Street (now Rocklin Road) as it looked prior to a fire in 1914. The Burchard Hotel is on the right. Businesses to the left of the hotel in the 1900s were Beasmore's Candies, Porter Saloon, a barbershop, livery stable, Porter Hall, Hislop Mortuary, West House and Kannasto Theatre, the Palace Oyster Bar and Chop House, Barudoni Market, Disano Saloon, and Scribner Store.

New York native James Burchard came to Placer County by 1867. He owned a saloon on bustling Front Street that in 1877 was destroyed by fire. He constructed his two-story hotel on the site of the old Rocklin Hotel. Burchard died in 1905, and the hotel was consumed in the 1914 fire.

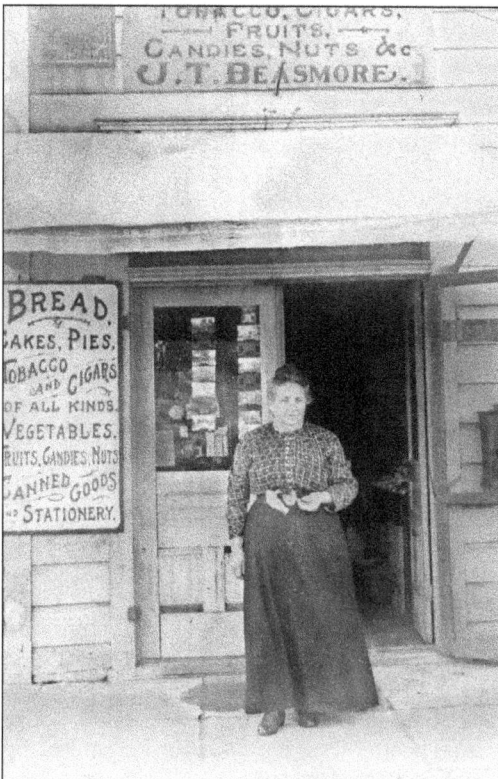

Mrs. Annie Beasmore stands in front of her candy store in 1910. John and Annie Beasmore came from Ireland and eventually settled in Rocklin. John worked in granite quarries and had a peach orchard on South Grove Street. After losing an arm in a quarry accident, he opened a small store next to the Burchard Hotel, where they worked until his death in 1908. Annie made it into a popular candy store and ice cream parlor.

In 1905, Swiss native Joseph Barudoni constructed this two-story building. The hoist on the left side of the structure lifted beef into the butcher shop and onto the rolling rack pictured below. The Echo Band celebrated the grand opening with free food, drink, and a concert.

Three butchers prepare meat in Barudoni's meat market. Sides of beef, hogs, and salami hang behind the butchers on a rack with rollers. Rocklin supported at least three butcher shops. DeWitt Porter had a meat market on the corner of Front and A Streets and J. Kenney near the roundhouse in 1895.

Butler Noles Scribner came to Rocklin from Tennessee in 1894. He opened this general merchandise business on Front Street that he operated until the railroad moved the roundhouse to Roseville. He then moved his business there and later became an insurance agent.

This view shows Front Street in 1907, looking north. The Barudoni building is on the left, trees adorn the front of the middle buildings, and Buchard's Hotel and the Central Pacific stone roundhouse is visible on the far right.

Rocklin had two major commercial streets—Front and Railroad Streets. Railroad Street, shown here in 1909, runs on the opposite side of the railroad tracks from Front Street. The Levison Store, on Railroad Street, can be seen in the right foreground. Also located on Railroad Street were the Pearson Bowling Saloon, Three Star Saloon, Holmes Saloon and Restaurant, Jennings Candy Store, Jodoin Barber Shop, the Southern Hotel, Dr. Woodbridge's office, F.A. Lewis's drug store, Curran Candy Store, a meat market, a rooming house, Pinsi Bakery, a tailor shop, Meade's shop, Freeman's hardware store, Freeman's undertaking parlor, and Ford's Store.

Isidor Levison, a native of Prussia, established a general merchandise business in the early 1870s. By 1879, Jacob Lesser Levison became a partner in the Levison Brothers store. In 1912, Alex Levison and Rose Morys pose on the porch of Levison's Store. The Masonic Hall was located upstairs. To the left is Pearson's Bowling Saloon, the Three Star Saloon, Holmes Saloon and Restaurant, and the Independent Order of Odd Fellows (IOOF) Hall.

The Levison store was first located on the corner of Front and Granite Streets (now Rocklin Road). After it burned in 1893, they moved the store to the brick building that had previously housed Mark Lavenson's store on Railroad Street. In 1895, Levison Brothers incorporated, with Jacob holding 249 shares, Isidore 248 shares, Hulda Levison 1 share, Emanuel Haines 1 share, and Henry Haines 1 share. The Masonic Hall (Granite Lodge No. 222) located on the upper floor was established in 1872.

The Cordova Saloon, pictured here sometime before 1914, doubled as a "chop house" restaurant. U.S. Holmes, who was killed in a shootout with Marshall Sam Renauldi on February 18, 1914, owned it. Renauldi also died after the showdown at Blackwell's Livery Stable on the southwest corner of Pacific Street and Rocklin Road. Next to the saloon is a coffee house and bakery that also housed a bathhouse and barbershop.

In this c. 1906 photo, a couple poses with a dog in front of a Wells Fargo & Company wagon. The Grand Southern Hotel is in the background on the upper right. The railroad passenger depot is the building on the upper left. "Gay Morgan" is written on the back of the picture, perhaps the name of the woman.

The Grand Southern Hotel is shown here in the left foreground. Next to the hotel was the Granite Saloon (owned by William Thompson), Charles Howser's barber shop, the Exchange Saloon (owned by J. C. Ackley), Mrs. C.L. Dunning's millinery shop, and the Masonic Hall, which housed Levison's Store.

The Grand Southern Hotel, located on the southeast corner of present-day Rocklin Road and Railroad Street, was known as the Western Hotel in 1907, when it was owned by E.L. Fellows. Only three names are listed on the back of this picture: Bob Larkin, Bill Larkin, and Will Crosby. Mr. Byyny managed the hotel at the time this picture was taken.

A group of old-timers stand in front of the Grand Southern Hotel in 1903. Listed on the back of the picture are Jack Kelley, John H. Riley, Bun Collins, Ed Fellows, Andy Jordan, George Glindcamp, ? Morgan, and Albert Nelson.

The quarry and railroad workers' medical needs were filled at the F.A. Lewis Drug Store (pictured here in 1905) and Smith and Knotwell's Drug Store on the northeast corner of Granite Street (now Rocklin Road) and Railroad Street, which had Dr. Stafford's office upstairs.

Samuel Trott owned Trott's Hotel, pictured here in 1877. The hotel was located on Railroad Street. It was primarily a boardinghouse for men who worked for the Central Pacific Railroad. In 1884, G.W. McCreedy owned the hotel and employed William Shaw as a dishwasher, William Ferrill as the cook, and Nellie Cunningham as a waitress. The building still stands at the northeast corner of Rocklin Road and Front Street.

Ford and Johnson opened their general merchandise store in the old Trott Hotel building. By 1920, it was a store with living quarters above, owned by Jack and Florence Kelley, and later Bottomley's Store. The post office is shown here in what was once the Davies Hotel building. The Davies Hotel, named for owner William Davies, was popular in the 1890s. Davies, a native of Wales, lived in Placer County in 1853.

Franklin Wesley Quast is pictured here with Peau Browning, postmistress Lena Gregory Dias, and George Neeley (in the buggy) in the early 1900s. F.W. Quast ran the Palace Meat Market in what was the old Davies Hotel building.

Two butchers stand ready to cut up some steaks in a Rocklin butcher shop. William Frederick Schuetze, a native of Prussia, came to Rocklin about 1868 and opened what was possibly the first butcher shop in Rocklin. In 1875, his place of residence was Franklin Store, probably the name of his shop. His nephew Carl Carpenter worked for William as a butcher, and his brother Albert was a butcher in nearby Penryn.

This 1905 view looks northwest toward the railroad tracks on Rocklin Road from the city hall. The Rocklin Bakery and Rocklin Rochdale Company's general merchandise store are visible on the right. Directors of the company included Peter Johnson, Ed Escola, Herman Lucki, Werner Leed, Thomas Hebuck, Matt Lehikolnen, and Emanuel Marttila. In 1913, burglars tried to dynamite the store's safe, which resulted in a large hole in the side of the building but left the safe unscathed. The same night, the store of the California Granite Company was also robbed. The thieves got $1.50 from the cash register.

The Rocklin Bakery and Grocery wagon waits for a load in front of the bakery in 1910. Names listed on the back of the picture are Mrs. Lekikonen, Hilma Kesti, and Bob and Hilfred Palo.

Bakers Soule and Nassi take bread out of the oven in the Rocklin Bakery. The Rocklin Rochdale Company operated the bakery. Rocklin boasted another bakery and confectionary (candy) shop, owned by Jacob Pfosi and Mrs. J.L. Curran, both located on Railroad Street.

Oscar W. Pekuri, a native of Finland, settled in Rocklin in 1907. He worked in the quarries for six years, including the time he spent managing the California Granite Company. He also worked as a clerk in Byyny's store for three years. In 1914, he opened his general merchandise store on Granite Street (now Rocklin Road) and ran it until the early 1930s.

Mr. Byyny, Oscar Pekuri, and Mr. Purdy stop working to pose for a picture in Mr. Byyny's store on the corner of Pacific Street and Rocklin Road.

This picture was taken inside Mary Fellows's store on Christmas Day in 1917. Two women, a baby in a buggy, and a child enjoy ice cream in the parlor in the back of the store while another woman shops in the front. Wooden crates of Cracker Jacks are stacked in the back right of the store. Note the Red Cross flag on the wall at right.

The Rocklin Public Works water wagon is loaded up and ready to supply residents with fresh mountain spring water hauled down from Blue Canyon in the Sierra Nevada Mountains by the Central Pacific Railroad. Residents of Rocklin stayed fairly free of typhoid, diphtheria, and other water-carried diseases by drinking the pure spring water.

Four

RESIDENTIAL ROCKLIN

This view of the Pete and Mike Johnson residence in Rocklin was probably captured around 1900. The Johnsons were one of the many Finnish families who came to Rocklin to work in the granite quarries. Pete Johnson owned a horse named Billy Jay and raced the horse at the Rocklin racetrack.

This picture of the Hurley home on the corner of Pacific and Oak Streets was taken right after the home was built. Pictured, from left to right, are (ground floor) Maggie Fry, Murial Selfridge, and Mike Hurley; (balcony) Katie Shatlee, Agnes Hurley, and Mabel Farrell.

A later picture of the Hurley home shows the growth of both foliage and family. Pictured, from left to right, are (front row) Katherine Hurley, Blanche Hurley, and Leland Hurley; (back row) Kate Hurley Smith, Agnes Hurley, and Zora Hurley.

This view shows the Hathaway house as it appeared in 1880. Pictured, from left to right, are Aaron Hathaway, Dora Hathaway, unidentified, Ardie ?, Father Hathaway, Sarah Grant, and Sadie Hayden. The Hathaways were one of the first families to settle in Rocklin. Aaron Hathaway leased a quarry in the 1880s and employed a large number of quarrymen.

The Talbot house is shown here around 1900. Pictured, from left to right, are Elise, Dan, and Nellie McKellips. The McKellips lived in the house from 1899 to 1904. Dan McKellips worked on the railroad.

In this early 1900s photo, Mrs. and Mr. Ben Nelson stand outside on the porch of their Rocklin home. It was reported in the 1887 *Argus* newspaper that the town of Rocklin had a curfew bell that would ring at 8 p.m. This bell signaled the tramps to leave town and the children to head home. The newspaper advised other towns to follow Rocklin's example.

This picture shows the Rasmussen home and family around 1897. Pictured, from left to right, are Harry, Christian, Roscoe, Andrew, and Boline. Christian Rasmussen came to Rocklin in 1889 as an engineer on the Central Pacific Railroad.

This picture of the Tom Newton home was snapped around 1900 with Floyd and Mrs. Newton on the porch. In the early 1900s, Rocklin's neighborhoods expanded. In 1904, J.S. Ryan, a Rocklin lumber merchant stated, "the building line has been booming in Rocklin for the past few months, and more buildings are going up than for many years previous."

This is the Charles Trott residence as it appeared before 1900. The house was sold to Dr. Pugg around 1900 and later burned down. The Trott's were very unlucky when it came to fires. Sam Trott, Charles Trott's father, owned the Trott Hotel. It caught on fire in 1869, and guest Henry Schmidt died in the conflagration.

This home, originally owned by the Palo family, was located on South Grove and Winding Lane. The picture, snapped around 1920, reveals tracks that went to a quarry. The Ruhkala family eventually owned the home.

Mike and Soffie Ruhkala's home was located on the southeast corner of High and Pine Streets. Mike's father built the home before 1919. Mike started his career as a stonecutter, but quit due to a hearing problem. He eventually went into the stock market and raised cattle.

The Aho home was located on the corner of High and Cedar Streets. The Aho family came from Finland and many of the Aho men worked in the quarries.

Pictured in front of the Anderson home, from left to right, are John, Lena, Selma, Bill, and Mr. and Mrs. Oscar Anderson. Oscar Anderson became a naturalized United States citizen in 1904.

This house just inside the gates to the Delano Quarry is pictured *c.* 1900. At one time, the Grindell family lived at the house. Ione Grindell Frederick taught second, third, and fourth grades at the Rocklin School in the 1920s. The house was moved away from the quarry on a hill, but was later destroyed by a fire.

Two unidentified women are pictured here in front the Jim Fisher home. The home faced the Delano Quarry. Jim Fisher worked at Delano Quarry and had a very short walk to work.

While working for the Southern Pacific Railroad, Dan McKellips roomed at this house owned by Mrs. Frick. He also stayed at the Davis Hotel, the old Ketchum House, the Southern Hotel, and Walter Braumman's home.

Two children are on the porch of the Grindell home on Second Street. Mr. Grindell was foreman of the California Granite Company and one of the oldest residents in the area. One of their daughters, Hazel Grindell, died at the age of 18 from tubercular meningitis in 1912.

Morse Mory, who ran a Railroad Street saloon called Mory's, had a home on High Street. Unfortunately, the saloon burned down in the fire of 1909, along with Dr. Ford's general store, Freeman's hardware store, Freeman's undertaking parlor, and others.

The Pernu home was located behind a store that later became the site of Rocklin City Hall. Mr. Pernu owned the California Granite Company. The Pernu home later burned down.

The Sonne home was located on an alley on Rocklin Road, just east of Pacific Street. The community of Rocklin worked to create a clean town. The *Placer Herald* announced in 1912 that March 19 was clean-up day and that "Five wagons have been donated and a house canvas will be made and all the rubbish will be hauled to the garbage dump which the city has furnished, back of the cemetery, out of the way of all public travel, and it is an ideal one, being an old abandoned quarry, and it will take a great many years to fill it up."

Pictured here is the Lehekonen's home, which was once the Neff home. On the back of the picture is recorded the following: Father, Mother, Imhi, and two unidentified friends of the Lehekonen family.

Pictured here *c.* 1900 is the Suhonen home, located on High Street. The people in the picture are unidentified. Although Rocklin was considered a bedroom community in the early 1900s, it did experience some crime. It was reported in a 1904 issue of the *Placer Herald* that Frank Clarke burglarized Forest Bradley's home.

A young boy is pictured in front of Mr. Byyny's home. Mr. Bynny managed the Southern Hotel and later owned a store on the corner of Rocklin and Taylor Roads. Mr. Byyny's store fell victim to fire in 1917 and was destroyed.

Five

RESIDENTS

Members of the local Rocklin Finnish fraternity gather for a picnic around 1915. Pictured, from left to right, are (front row) Victor Sandel, Ancel Hooga, August Pakola, Matt Palo, Ensti Koskela, Sanfred Wallen, Sam Kesti, ? Friberg, John Pisila, and ? Nayki; (second row) John Kauppi, Matt Hacobson, Anthi Komulainen, Oscar Eleason, Adolf Larson, Emmanuel Martila, Matt Oja, John Kannasto, John Jarvis, August Hill, and Mike Ruhkala; (third row) ? Matson, Esa Palo, Gabriel Alexson, unidentified, Charles Weissenfelt, Hames Annalla, "Gold Ike" Issac, John Wallen, ? Kokila, unidentified, Adolf Pernu, Sefanias Hendrickson, and Gus Halonen; (back row) unidentified, August Sippola, John Lauri, Henry Parkkinen, Mike Johnson, Tom Hebuck, Matt Lehikoinen, Elias Eliason, ? Hebuck, unidentified, Oscar Anderson, and Sakri Hendrickson.

Pictured here are Matt and Lusina Oja. Matt was encouraged to come to America to work in the Rocklin quarries by John Mantyla and other Finnish families, and he did. Many of the Finnish, once arriving in Rocklin, would write back home about the plentiful work and the beautiful town.

Matt Oja, a member of the Rocklin Echo Band, poses for a picture. In addition to playing in the Echo Band and working at a quarry, Matt also belonged to the Rocklin Finnish Fraternity.

Dr. Fletcher sits for a formal portrait.
The *Placer Herald* reported in April 1916
that five new automobiles were purchased
in Rocklin. Dr. Fletcher was recorded as
the latest person to purchase the new
"Tin Lizzie."

Mr. and Mrs. William Maki pose for this
portrait. William Maki was born in Wiha
Kyra, Finland, in 1886. He became a
naturalized citizen of the United States
in 1914.

Lillie Rosina Mullough was the wife of Charles Cornelius Trott. Her son Charles was a railroad man.

Charles Cornelius Trott, a storeowner and former railroad man, was born in Volcano, California, on December 12, 1855.

In 1893, at the age of 24, Matt Ruhkala poses for a formal portrait. He was born in Kalajoki, Finland, and came to Rocklin in 1889. His first wife, Lizzie Piippola, and their only child are buried at the west end of the Rocklin cemetery. He married his second wife, Eva Erickson, in 1901 and had 11 children: Miriam, Rachel, Abner, Michael, Benjamin, Ruben, Elizabeth, Ruth, Roy, Marshall, and Margaret.

This striking early 20th-century portrait of a young Rocklin woman wearing a dress with leg o'mutton sleeves may be of Lillian "Lillie" Clinton Scribner. She was married to Butler Scribner and had two children, Howard and Benton. Lillie was born in 1870 and passed away in 1949.

Butler Scribner was born in Tennessee in 1872 and came to Rocklin in 1894. He opened a general mercantile on Front Street. When the roundhouse was moved to Roseville, he followed and opened a store in Roseville. Butler owned three horses that he raced at the Rocklin racetrack. One of the horses, Lady S. Scribner, died in 1942.

Pictured, from left to right, are (front row) three unidentified boys, Tom Elliot, two unidentified boys, Myrtle Blackwill, unidentified girl, Lena Newhert and son, J. Allen, Laura Willard, unidentified , Helen Blackwill, Helen Hislop, Etta Tuttle, unidentified, Margaret Elliot, unidentified, Marie Hebuck, and Ione Grindell; (middle row) Hiraru Grindell, unidentified boy, Ed Lithtola, Mrs. Hislop, Nell Neff, Lena Rinaldi, Ella Wilson, Mrs. Watters, Clara Rinaldi with three young girls, Mrs. Huley, Susie Ross, Mrs. Willard with Mrs. Ousal in front of her, Mrs. Kelley, Mrs. Norton, and Susie Gregoug; (back row) ? Wheeler, Irving Elliot, Mrs. Ross Sr., Mrs. Clough, unidentified woman, Bill Huley and child, Bobbie Trick, Mrs. Brenton, Miss Sharp, Mrs. Moore with Norton, and Mrs. Allen.

John Tiitu and Mrs Salo dressed in Finnish costume for a play at Porters Hall around 1913. Porters Hall was located on Front Street between the livery stable and Hislop Mortuary. The hall burned down in the 1914 fire.

Three young men, Taino Kokkila, Eino Nassi, and Lauri Pentila, enjoy a picnic in 1914. Many local Rocklin boys played for the Rocklin baseball team, including Taino Kokkila, who played for the local team in the 1910s.

John Kannasto and his family came to Rocklin in the 1890s. John worked for the quarries and eventually opened a movie theater. The movie theater burned down in the 1914 fire. Later, Mrs. Kannasto and her daughters opened an ice cream parlor.

Sigrid Lehtola is pictured here in 1915. The Lehtola family came from Finland.

Pictured here in the early 1900s are brother and sister Anders Oscar Wickman and Hilda Wickman Pekuri. A.O. Wickman came to Rocklin in 1890 and worked as a quarryman. He eventually ran a quarry and was mayor of Rocklin for several years. Hilda was the wife of Oscar Pekuri, a granite worker, shop owner, and dairy owner.

Aino Aho Luoma poses with her child c. 1912. Her relative, Alexsanderi Luoma, was born in Jurva, Finland, in 1882. He became a United States citizen in 1921.

Many men from Finland came to Rocklin to work in the granite industry and often joined the Finnish fraternity. This group is just a fraction of the fraternity members. Pictured, from left to right, are (front row) Adolph Larson and Matt Lehikoinen; (back row) Richard Kesti, Ivar Kesti, and an unidentified man.

Mr. and Mrs. A.C. Henry and their child, Culberson, pose for a formal portrait.

Pictured is Alberta Palo Jensen, daughter of Art and Ina Palo. She was born in Rocklin about 1920. The Palos were from Finland and came to Rocklin to work in the quarries.

Photographer Burton Hodson, captured Tom and Ina Hebuck in what was probably a wedding portrait. Tom was the brother of Henry Hebuck, a quarry owner. Tom and Ina moved back to Finland when the quarry industry declined.

Although there was a large Finnish population in Rocklin, some of the other early settlers were Irish. There was also a large Chinese population. Many of the Chinese came to Rocklin to work on the railroads. According to Roy Ruhkala, a Rocklin native and an authority on Rocklin history, 1876 there was a "Chinatown" behind the roundhouse.

Nicholai "Nick" Alexson worked on a quarry with his father, Gabriel Alexson and, eventually, owned a quarry with Vic Wickstrom. Gabriel Alexson came from Finland and became a naturalized citizen in 1894.

Pictured here are Mr. and Mrs.
Lissi Kleimolalle.

John George Tiitu poses in front of the Morttila house in 1917. Tiitu was born in Lapua,
Finland, in 1888. He officially became a citizen of the United States on May 7, 1914.

The Hill family from Finland poses for a family portrait. The back of the portrait identifies Helmi Hill (in back) and Eino Hill (holding the flag).

Two men stand in a citrus grove in Rocklin in 1906. The *Placer Herald* reported in 1912 that "A welcome rain has at last arrived and the farmers are correspondingly happy. Quite a large acreage here is planted to hay and grain and the soil was getting pretty dry."

This cabinet card photograph features two Rocklin residents, an unidentified mother and child, in a formal portrait. Popular in the late 1800s, cabinet cards have three key characteristics: they are printed on bristol board or cardstock, gilded, and the photographer's name and location are printed on the front of the card.

Pictured, from left to right, are Lem Purdy, Tom Farrell, Walter Sandell, Joe Dias, and Alex Levison. The picture was taken c. 1915. Joe Dias married Lena Olive Gregory, the Rocklin postmistress, in May 1913. Lena Gregory Dias's father, John Gregory, was Rocklin's city clerk. Joe and Lena were well liked in the community and popular among their peers.

The boys in this picture are identified on the back of the photograph as Bill Hurley (sitting on the railing) and Vic Wickstrom (standing on the steps). They came from two of the earliest Finnish families that worked in the quarries in the Rocklin.

John Mantyla, born 1857 in Jurva, Finland, came to Rocklin around 1875. Not only did he bring the first eucalyptus trees to Rocklin, he also created the explosion in Rocklin's Finnish population. He encouraged his fellow countrymen to join him and helped more Finnish become owners of quarries. His home on Granite Street, near the current city hall, was considered a showplace for roses, lilacs, and other spring flowers. In 1906, he sold all of his belongings and left Rocklin.

Six

SCHOOL AND CHURCH

Rocklin School students assemble for a picture on December 20, 1912. Rocklin School District was formed in August 1866 with Miss Ellen Hinckley as the first teacher. By the 1880s the district had a primary and a grammar school. By 1881 students numbered over 120 and the library contained 106 volumes. In 1883, the two-story schoolhouse with four classrooms, two on each story, was constructed.

Pictured *c.* 1901 is Miss Mollie E. Norton's class at Rocklin School. From left to right, they are (front row) Walter Campbell, John Cronin, Alf Layton, Charles Clough, George Shroder, Lewis Hebuck, John Freeman, Ethel Allen, Iva Porter, and unidentified; (back row) Myrtle Clough, Alice Sheehan, Anna Purdy, Myrtle Landis, Miss Mollie E. Norton, Mary Freeman, Beatrice Whitney, Hazel Crosby, Hazel Willard, Anna Horner, Ethel Mills, Leonard Layton, and Willie Tuttle.

Mrs. Annie Plummer's primary school class, from left to right, are (front row) Sulo Hebuck, Bob Larkins, Danny Wright, Milton Williams, Della Mata Nielson, Henry Halonen, Walter Halonen, Myron McKay, John Hurly, Peter Johnson, Jesse Fisher, Herbert Landis, Alfred Willard, Earl Murray, Roy ?, Lembert Purdy, Milton Williams, Raymond Layton, Eugene Tuttle, Lewis Tuttle, Fay Ingram, and Fred Johnson; (second row) Isabel Gomez, Mamie Morys, Eddie Freeman, Joe Gomez, Arthur Browning, Joe Ponce, Ester Levinson, Lewis Ruth, Fanny Matson, Tony Eglesias, Clarence Neff, and Earl Jeardeau; (third row) Tara Ponce, Ted Gooding, Joe Gomez, Hugh Owens, Howard Tox, Erma Udbye, Roscoe Schifler, Emil Bush, Lottie Gannon, Andy Jordan, Mabel Farrell, Nellie Blower, Mamie Uieb, John Lonergan, Oscar Clater, Walter ?, and June Browning; (back row) Etta Davis, ? Davis, Katie Hurley, ? Crother, Emma De Sano, Arlie Annabel, Ray Annabel, Anita Grindell, Rita Grindell, "Goddess of Liberty," Christine Parker, Helmi Hill, Nettie Ponce, Kupie Ponce, Charles Soule, Hazel Isoard, Hattie Tuttle, Nellie Roberts, Emma Sparks, and Edna Hoenen.

Mr. Carl Phillipi's 1903 grammar school class consisted of seventh-graders Alfred Layton, Willie Crosby, Mary Udbye, Ethel Mills, Anna Woodbridge, Walter Campbell, Hazel Willard, Iva Porter, Mary Freeman, Isabelle Rugg, George Shroder, Agnes Prosser, Beatrice Whitney, and Alice Lee. The eighth grade students were Dick Ross, Hattie Tuttle, Myrtle Clough, Bessie Haley, Henry Curran, Jessie Smith, Pauline Ruth, Alice Udbye, Lottie Purdy, Mildred Delano, Gladys Landis, Maud Prosser, and Floyd Newton. Ninth grade students were Anna Purdy, Alice Sheehan, Myrtle Landis, Jay Franchy, and John Freeman.

The 1907 graduating class poses for a picture. From left to right are (front row) Ester Levinson, Gladys Eyer, Edna Prosser, Hilma Hill, Laura Campbell, Margie Jeardeau, Mabel Farrell, and Anita Grindell; (back row) Ava Whallen, Nellie Roberts, Flossie Davis, Nina Gebhardt, Lois Blackwell, and the teacher, Mr. F.T. Murman, seated in the middle.

Mrs. Betts's class is shown here c. 1907. Pictured, from left to right, are (front row) Albion Escola, Emile Lehtola, Carl Fredericks, Leland Ayers, William Prosser, Richard Walden, John Anderson, Louis Aho, Jolen Sheehan, and Gust Halonen; (second row) Rita Larkin, Cora Butler, Lempi Alexson, Amelia Beecroft, Gertrude Bailey, Bertha Bradley, Mabel Gebhardt, Hilma Ruhkala, and Evelyn Hambly; (third row) Sadie Roberts, Senia Jacobson, Emma Hytinen, Allie Haken, Lempi Hebuck, Wilfred Leggett, Burton Scoon, Lawrence Lonergan, Sumner Rugg, and Irwin Elliott; (back row) Lillian Hambine, Alta Lovejoy, Rosemary Healey, Jean Ayers, Maggie Farrell, Hilda Johnson, and Ruby Battenfield.

The fourth-grade class of 1908 stands on the steps of the Rocklin School. Pictured, from left to right, are (front row) ? Ketcham, Uno Hebuck, Jack Clinton, Warren Lovejoy, Oscar Hutala, John Morys, unidentified, and Milton Kinkler; (second row) Willis Ayer, Henry Nelson, Eddie Lehtola, Eugene Field, Paul Udby, Ernest Willard, ? Holmes, and Howard Scribner; (third row) Albert Halonen, Henry Klemp, Henry Lucas, Charles Purdy, Florence Ketcham, unidentified, Aili Hill, and Blanche Garrett; (back row) Lempi Hendrickson, Zeta Whallen, Marie Elliott, Ida Johnson, Sybil Moore, Regina Nelson, Mabel Gregory, and Alice Wickman.

The 1912 sixth- and seventh-grade classes pose for a picture on the steps of the school. Pictured, from left to right, are (front row) Mary Hebuck, Laura Willard, Viola Bradley, Walter Barnes, Everett Wheeler, Susie Gregory, Alfred Nassi, and Eino Halonen; (back row) Muriel Laird, Bessie Broach, Impi Ester Pisila, Ione Grindell, Jane Allen, Gertrude Bradley, Benton Scribner, and Ernest Willard.

Miss Brown's primary class of 1912 gathers for a picture at the side of Rocklin School. Students listed on the back of photograph are Alec Alexson, Clarence Mehl, Albert Johnson, Arthur Bradley, Carl Ojala, Oscar Halonen, Roy Nettle, Otto Ojala, Abian Pisila, Joe Gregory, John Emerson, Arvo Minkkinen, LeRoy Hendrickson, Lurley Jackson, Etta Tuttle, Ada Bolton, Selma Johnson, Ann Striberg, Lillie Wallen, Wilford Palo, Arvie Hebuck, Siiri Hukkinen, Helen Hislop, Zelma Klemp, Bertha Bradley, ? Wickman, Anita York, Tunie Whallen, Lena Kesti, Charlie Pernu, Hazel York, Rachel Ruhkala, Alma Nassi, Jennie Byyny, Marguerite Elliott, Frances Marx, Thelma Heitala, and Jennie Whallen.

The Rocklin teachers pictured in this c. 1913 photo are, from left to right, Mrs. Amanda Sharpe, Miss Hansen, Mr. P.J. Jacobs, Miss Brown, and Miss Effie Tripp. Those who taught between 1895 and 1904 and are not pictured here include C.S. Taylor, Mrs. B. Cromwell, Belle Bankhead, Maybelle McKay, W.S. Cranmer, Edith Leinbach, Wilhelmina Wendt, Eva Rose Schnider, and Mrs. M.M. Scoon.

The 1913 graduating class lines up for a picture, possibly in the yard of the Wickmans, who owned a quarry in Rocklin. Graduates, from left to right, are Alfred Nassi, Laura Willard, Muriel Laird, Impi Ester Pisila, Mr. P.E. Jacobs, Jennebelle Allen, Bertha Bradley, Ione Grindell, Eino Halonen, and Gertrude Bradley.

96

Rocklin students are photographed prior to a May Day celebration in front of the maypole. The girls, from left to right, are (front row) Hilma Kesti, Ester Ruhkala, Nora Morse, and Tillie Jacobson; (back row) Helen Johnson, Minnie Wickman, Ino Palo, Lena Anderson, Hannah Virta, Ida Kennedy, Elma Kannasto, and Effie Anderson.

Rocklin girls stop for a picture during the maypole dance. Pictured, from left to right, are Tillie Jacobson, Ino Palo, Effie Anderson, Helen Johnson, Ester Ruhkala, Ida Kennedy, Lena Anderson, Minnie Wickman, Elma Kannasto, Hannah Virta, Hilma Kesti, and Nora Morse.

This Lutheran confirmation class is pictured c. 1920 in their Sunday best. The girls, from left to right, are (front row) Gertrude Aho, Viena Wickman, Elma Minkkinen, and Mary Hagman; (middle row) Helen Kesti, Martha Nassi, and Edna Whallen; (back row) ? Liikola,? Hagman, Torni Palo, John Palo, minister, Albert Kannasto, Abe Nassi, ? Liikola, and Rudolph Ruhkala.

St. Mary's Church of the Assumption, located on Front Street, was dedicated in August 1883. Organized in 1881, the Rocklin Catholic congregation began fundraising for a church building at a St. Patrick's Day dance. The steeple was taken down because of damage by woodpeckers. Though the structure is in very poor condition, it is still standing after 120 years.

This Congregational Church was built in 1895, replacing the one constructed in 1883. The Congregational Society incorporated in 1884 with William Bankhead, Charles Rowel, R. Rowel, and R.A. Mills elected to the board of directors for that year. Others present at the meeting were G.L. Stuff; S.J. Taylor; Lily, Lydia, James and Emma Addicott; Mr. and Mrs. Morrison; J. Good, Eva Wolley, Charles Philbrick, George Wilker, and Rev. J.H. Warren.

The Methodist Episcopal Church of Rocklin was located on Lot 11 on Third Street. James Bolton sold the lot to the church for $100 in 1869. The new church, pictured here, was constructed in 1893. Rocklin also had two Lutheran churches—one located at the junction of Winding Lane and Lost Avenue, the other on South Grove Street.

Finnish Labor Temple, occupying the former Methodist church building, was established in 1914. The following year quarry workers went on strike, while the town was still reeling from the devastating fire of 1914. The strike dealt a powerful blow to Rocklin quarries and many quarry workers had moved to Porterville and Raymond. Even prominent quarries failed to reopen after the strike. At this time, Delano's quarry was sold to the City of Rocklin for a mere $10 for use as a dumpsite.

The interior of the Finnish Labor Temple is decorated for a play on January 10, 1914. The temple was located on Rocklin Road between San Francisco and High Streets. It was torn down in the 1930s.

Seven

ENTERTAINMENT

The Finnish National Temperance Association built Rocklin's Finnish Temperance Hall in 1905. The association hired George Gilmore of Loomis, California, to build "Finn Hall." Although he started building in 1904, a strong wind blew down the exterior walls, forcing him to start again. It has been rumored that poor George lost money on this project.

This scene was captured around 1912. Hilma Kesti and Aili Dondrick sit on the bicycle on the right side of the picture. Not long after Finn Hall was built, Mrs. Hill spotted a fire inside the building. Luckily, it was quickly put out and the only damage was a hole in the hardwood floor. Finn Hall was able to escape the devastating fires that plagued Rocklin throughout its history.

A group of builders work on Finn Hall in 1904. The platform and circular steps at the entrance are made of Rocklin granite, which local quarries generously donated. Local craftsmen cut all of the granite needed for free.

A glimpse inside the Finn Hall in 1915 reveals a wonderful community space. According to Roy Ruhkala, "Since the hall was built, practically every function that took place in Rocklin was held at the Finn Hall."

Finn Hall (or "Finish Hall" [sic]) is decorated for a grammar school graduation. The hall was host to the Rocklin Grammar School graduation from 1905 until 1952 and also hosted a variety of performances and festivities, including concerts and plays.

Rockliners travel by rail on a July 3, 1903 Lake Tahoe excursion. This well-dressed group enjoyed the convenience of the railroad that practically stopped at their doorsteps and took them throughout Placer County and beyond. By 1932, when industry and commerce had declined, the train would stop in Rocklin only if it was flagged down, and in 1938 the depot was torn down.

A group pauses for a picture inside the Lake Tahoe excursion train around 1902. Rocklin was also a destination for excursion trains. The Central Pacific Railroad maintained a beautiful park, and people would come from miles around for summer picnics.

Horses and horse racing were sources of entertainment and pride for many in Rocklin. A racetrack was built in 1893, and people from all over Placer County and Northern California came to race their horses. This picture was probably taken in the early 1900s.

Rocklin residents gather near the racetrack around 1907. Mr. Bynny and Lembert Purdy are seated in the buggy. The horse's name was Bird. The racetrack was used for harness racing, horse racing, and, eventually, motorcycle races.

A covered grandstand is packed for the races in 1901. A group of residents formed the Rocklin Driving Park Association in 1895 to encourage the breeding of thoroughbreds and superior horses, as well as to conduct speed contests, racing meetings, and agricultural fairs. Some of the first directors of the association were John Sweeney, W.C. Delano, J.L. Levison, and John T. Whitney.

Henry Hebuck poses with his horse Moka Boy around 1905. Henry and Moka Boy entered as many sulky horse races as possible.

Alongside his horse Jewess, Alex Levison shows off his trophy for winning a race. Jewess ran the one mile in 2:15 on the Rocklin track.

Harvey Blackwell prepares for a harness race with his horse Golden State in 1912. The tall building in the back was a drugstore, the closest small building was Dr. Fletcher's office, and the stone building was part of the old roundhouse.

Sam Hendrickson poses in 1912 with Golden State, a horse co-owned by Sam Hendrickson and Harvey Blackwell. Horses were very valuable and even became the object of lawsuits. The *Placer Herald* reported in 1904 that J.M. O'Keefe sued J. Barudoni for damages to a horse. O'Keefe was awarded $25.

The Levison brothers, shown above *c.* 1900, owned six shares in the Rocklin Driving Park Association. J.L. Levison was also a director of the association. Another director was the postmaster, Joe Hackett, who doubled as the bookmaker for the racetrack.

Pictured here, from left to right, are Joe Dias, Jack Jordan, and Alf Willard. Joe Dias worked in the quarries as an oiler. Alf Willard was the son of George Willard, a granite cutter for the Rocklin Granite Company.

John Jarvi, a quarryman, loved horses and poses on a sulky with one of his horses. He worked in Matt Ruhkala's quarry for many years. Races were always well attended, and in 1912 the *Placer Herald* reported, "The matinee of the Rocklin Driving Club on the afternoon of the Fourth of July was attended by a large crowd who were entertained by a fine program of races and kindred spirits."

A group of young men travels on horseback through Rocklin. Pictured, from left to right, are Harry Bradley, Jack Jordan, and two unidentified boys.

An unidentified man lifts Adolph Larson. The two gentlemen belonged to an athletic club. Many Rocklin citizens were involved in recreational sports and the town was promoted as a healthy place to live. Visitors to Rocklin remarked that the town, with its clean fresh air, was a good place to recover from an illness.

Adolph Larson poses in his Rocklin Athletic League uniform. Larson came to Rocklin from Finland and eventually returned there.

A group of Rocklin men enjoy a rousing game of football. Rocklin was well known in Placer County for the sports prowess of its citizens.

The Rocklin baseball team and champions of Placer County of 1906 included Jim Lee, Howard Fox, Roscoe Shuler, ? Anderson, Jake Pofer, Lee Tudsbury, Wallis Condon, Charles Halonen, Foster Bradley, Bert Farrell, and Jim Tulley. The *Placer Herald* often covered the games between Placer County baseball teams. In a 1902 article, it was reported after a six to five loss to Folsom that:

> A close and exciting game of ball took place at Rocklin Sunday before a large and enthusiastic crowd. All the fans from Newcastle, Folsom, and surrounding towns were out in full force. It was anybody's game until the last man was out. It was Rocklin's initial game and the boys were a little nervous and made some costly errors in the second inning, which virtually gave Folsom the game. Bolz, Rocklin's new pitcher, is a machinist in the shops there. He is just out from Topeka, Kansas. He pitched first class ball and fielded his position in good shape, having two put-outs and five assists, which is quite a record for a pitcher.

Larry Hendrickson and Henry Hebuck pose in their baseball uniforms. The April 8, 1916 issue of the *Placer Herald* states:

> The uniforms for the Rocklin baseball team arrived this week, and are very natty-gray with green trimmings. The boys are practicing faithfully every day and it is expected that a game will be played Sunday, but the opposing team has not been decided on. The grounds have been fixed up in good shape, the diamond scraped and the outfield leveled up. If the new league materializes, Rocklin is ready. If not, independent games will be played all summer and the secretary is besieged with offers of teams to come here and play. 'Home talent!' why Rocklin has them all beat to a frazzle on that point. Every member of the team was either born here or came here when they were infants, and we have enough of them to make two teams.

The Rocklin boys of summer played teams as far away as Sacramento. In 1914, Rocklin beat the Sacramento Cascades nine to four. The Rocklin team played home games in a rented vacant lot behind the old roundhouse, where they set up a baseball diamond. This field was used until the late 1920s.

Pictured here is one of the players for the Rocklin team, Eugene "Del" Alexson. In the early days of Rocklin baseball, many of the players were also quarrymen. Del's father owned a quarry.

Members of the Rocklin Owls, pictured from left to right, are (front row) Stanley Cain, unidentified, Bob Palo, Arvo Minkkinen, Sulo Hebuck, Larry Hendrickson, Alex H., and Emil Sukonen; (back row) Wayne Minkkinen, Dave Roderick, Alex Alenson, Steve ?, unidentified, Aino Hebuck, and Toivo Niskala.

A group of young baseball players get ready for a game in 1905. Most of the boys were sons of railroad workers and quarrymen. Before the baseball diamond was set up behind the old roundhouse, they used a baseball diamond inside the Rocklin Racetrack.

Hopsburger Beer sponsored the Rocklin baseball team of 1914. The picture was taken in front of Mrs. West's house and some of the men in front are identified. The second man on the left is Charley Halonen, the pitcher. Sulo Hebuck is the third man on the left, and the fourth man on the on the left is "Del" Alexson. Walter Halonen is the third man on the right. The team of 1914 played Auburn at the Auburn Recreation District Park and the *Placer Herald* reported, "the fielding of the home team was ragged and seven of them contributed to the error column. About 175 people witnessed the slaughter of the home team. Below is the score. 'Nough said." The score was Rocklin 11, Auburn 0.

A small crowd watches the Rocklin women's basketball team play a Sacramento team c. 1913.

Rocklin's 1914 women's basketball squad poses for their team picture.

Six members of the 1913 women's basketball team commemorate their season with a snapshot. Pictured, from left to right, are (front row) Susie Gregory, Eula Rugg, and Gertrude Bradley; (back row) Bertha Bradley, Henna Virta, and Jennebelle Allen.

Pictured, from left to right, are Edna Alexson, Nick Alexson, Anna Palo, and Epa Palo. The two couples are enjoying the first annual Roseville Fair in 1915. Both Nick Alexson and Epa Palo were quarrymen.

118

Nikolas "Nick" Alexson played in the Rocklin Band in the early 1900s. Alexson came to America from Finland when he was four years old. He worked in the quarries and co-owned a company that was respected for its cutwork.

Nikolai Alexson

The Rocklin Echo Band plays in front of the Rocklin Railroad Depot on June 30, 1907. The man in the middle in the front row is Matt Oja. The Echo Band was hired to play during races and between innings at baseball games at the Rocklin Racetrack.

This c. 1900 image shows members of the Rocklin Band, frequently hired to play at picnics and celebrations.

The brass section of the Echo Band of Rocklin poses for a picture at one of the many public picnics in Rocklin around 1907. Matt Oja is on the right.

In 1913, the Rocklin Band competed against a few Bay Area bands during a picnic sponsored by the Finnish Socialist Societies. Unfortunately for Rocklin, the Berkeley brass band took first prize.

The Finns of Rocklin often organized big family picnics near China Gardens. The band would play, and games and competitions of all kinds abounded.

The surnames of old-timers of the Finnish Brotherhood Lodge pictured, from left to right, are (front row) Ruhkala, Laurie, Hendrickson, Jacobson, Hendrickson, Wickman, Sandel, Alexson, Escola, Ourni, and Hooga; (middle row) Aho, Mattila, Kesti, Sanobel, Hendrickson, Elaison, Hietola, and Hubuck; (back row) Wallen, Hill, Naykkii, Pisela, Pakola, Halonen, and Anderson.

A few men outside the bar at Buchard's look like they are up to no good on a fine afternoon in Rocklin. From bands to baseball to beer, Rocklin provided many entertainment options to its railroad workers, quarrymen, and others.

Eight

FIRE

ROCKLIN FIRE HOUSE, 1904
1904

Fire was a constant threat to the people of Rocklin. Before the establishment of the Rocklin Hose Company in 1894, the town suffered several devastating fires that left them powerless to save the many businesses that were incinerated. Members of the all-volunteer hose company paid $2 to join and monthly dues for the honor and opportunity to carry out the duties of a fireman. This picture shows the Rocklin Hose Company building, which was also used as the city hall.

At the beginning of the 20th century, Rocklin's Front Street saw a boom in building and businesses. At a cost of about $6,000, the Fireman's Hall was built in 1905. Unfortunately, a fire in 1906 destroyed this hall along with the homes of Henry Mullnix and John Lonergan.

This photo shows a fire breaking out at the racetrack in Rocklin. During the fire of 1914 that destroyed most of Rocklin's Front Street businesses, the races did not stop. The May 9, 1914 *Placer Herald* reported that "The races in the afternoon were well attended, considering the big fire that was raging in town."

The fire of 1914 began around 1 p.m. in Porter's old livery stable. The 200 tons of hay that Chester Purdy stored there just invited fire, although rumor has it that someone saw a group of kids smoking the stable just before the fire broke out.

Sadly, the fire that occurred on May 8, 1914, wiped out most of the businesses and a few homes on Front Street. To make matters worse, just five years earlier in 1909, a fire leveled many businesses on Railroad Street. Rocklin saw the future of their town literally go up in flames.

FIRE ROCKLIN. CAL. MAY 8 1914

The *Placer Herald* reported this account of the fire:

A strong wind was blowing and the firemen were helpless. Everything from Bardooni's [sic] butcher shop to the post office was totally destroyed. Sparks were carried to other parts of town, destroying two dwellings. Three fire engines from Roseville were on hand, looking after the railroad company's property. One of them kept a stream on the post office and succeeded on saving it after it had been on fire a half dozen times. Postmaster Hackett had all the contents of the office removed to a place of safety. Following are the losses as neat as could be ascertained: Dan Hart, saloon property, $500; James Clark building, $2,500; Mullinix building, $1000; Colin Hislop, tenant, undertaking parlors, $500; Mrs. Beasmore, rooms, $250; Porter building, $3000; Beasmore and Johnson, saloon, $1000; Chester Purdy, hay, $2500; Burchard Hotel, $5000; Palo and Tilson, saloon, $1000; Levison building, $2500; C.D. Sweetman, saloon, $1000; A.B. Lovejoy, dwelling, $500; A.D. Cartwright, dwelling, $500; Musser and Johnson, saloon, $1000.

Very few of the buildings destroyed by the fires of 1909 and 1914, shown here, were rebuilt. Only a few years before, business had boomed, buildings of stature were built, and promising rumors of a larger railroad roundhouse to come hinted at a bright future. Rocklin took decades to recover after the fires and the relocation of the roundhouse to Roseville.

Townspeople and firefighters attempt to keep the fire from spreading to every business on Front Street. Through heroic efforts, the post office was saved. The Barudoni building, housing a butcher shop, also survived the flames.

The people of Rocklin view the devastation caused by the fire on May 8, 1914. Many destroyed businesses were not insured. The *Placer Herald* lamented, "The hotel was insured for $1,500, Mrs. Beasmore for $800, and Purdy hay was about all the insurance carried, as the rate was too high and the insurance companies did not want it." The fire nearly ended the city of Rocklin. The next year, a granite workers' strike caused many quarries to close. Long-established businesses finally gave up and moved to Roseville or closed. And that was not the end of the conflagrations—two fires engulfed the town again in 1922. Rocklin, once the second largest city in Placer County, almost disappeared. Yet not unlike a phoenix, Rocklin was reborn out of the ashes and, in the 1960s, it saw a resurgence of population and development. Today, Rocklin is one of the fastest-growing towns in California.

www.ingramcontent.com/pod-product-compliance
Lightning Source LLC
Chambersburg PA
CBHW050546110426
42813CB00008B/2271